Out Yc

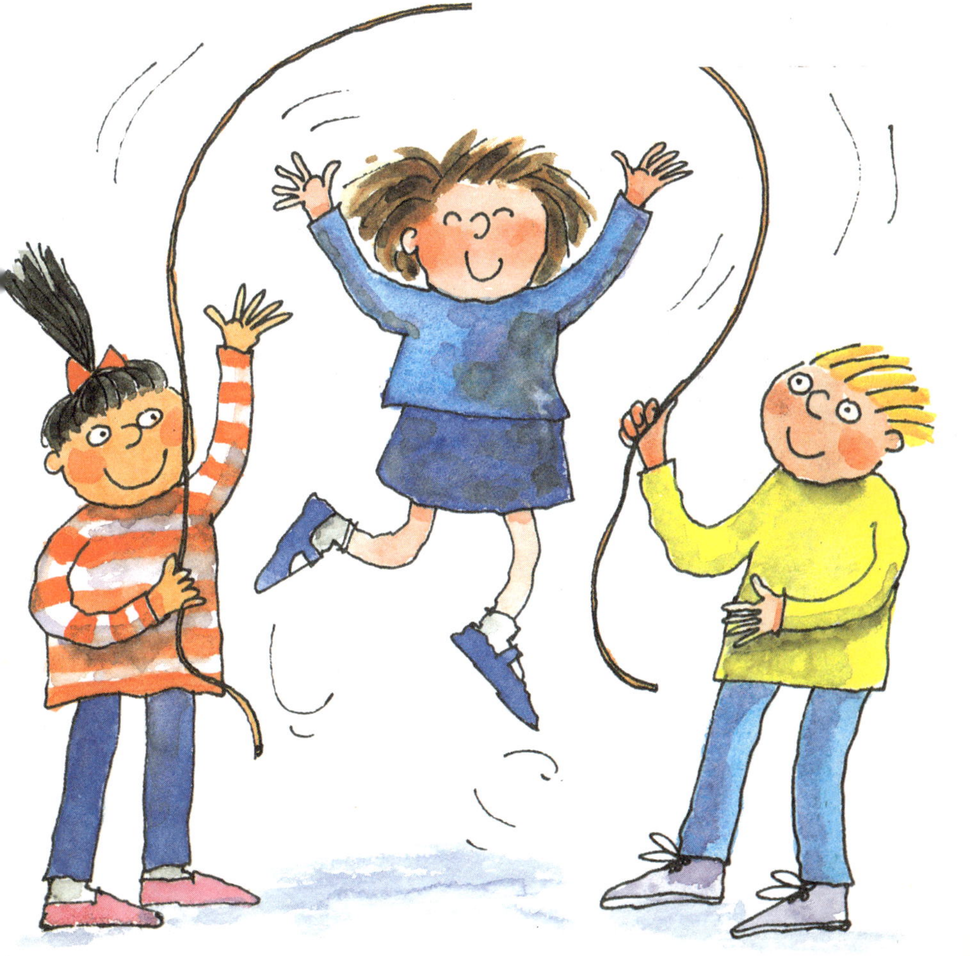

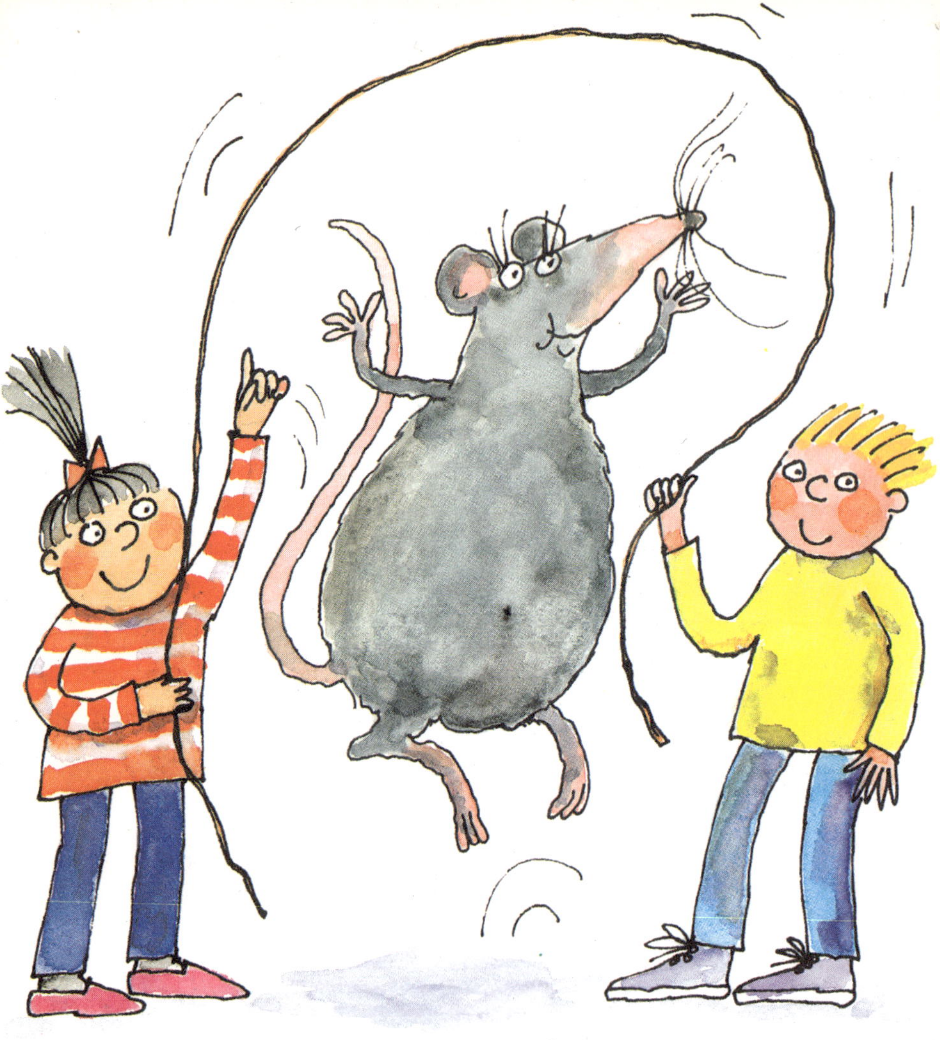

Out goes the rat.

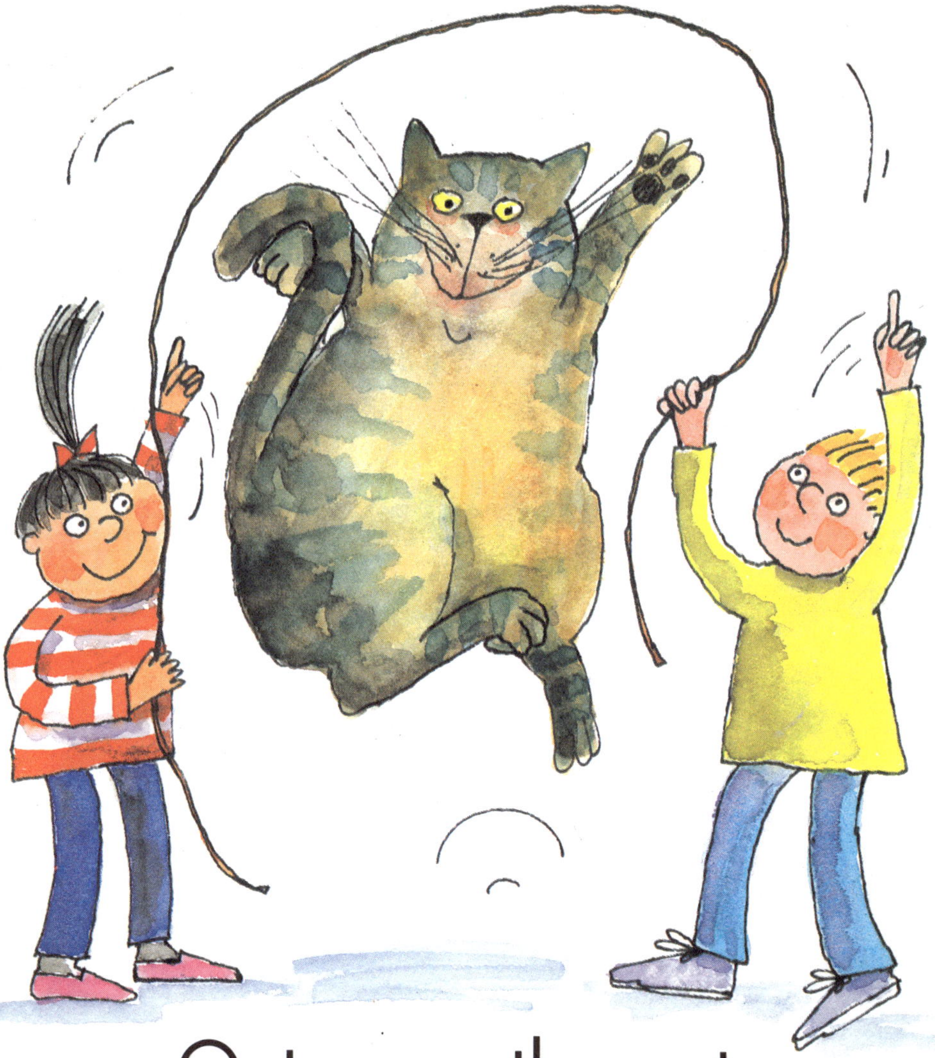

Out goes the cat.

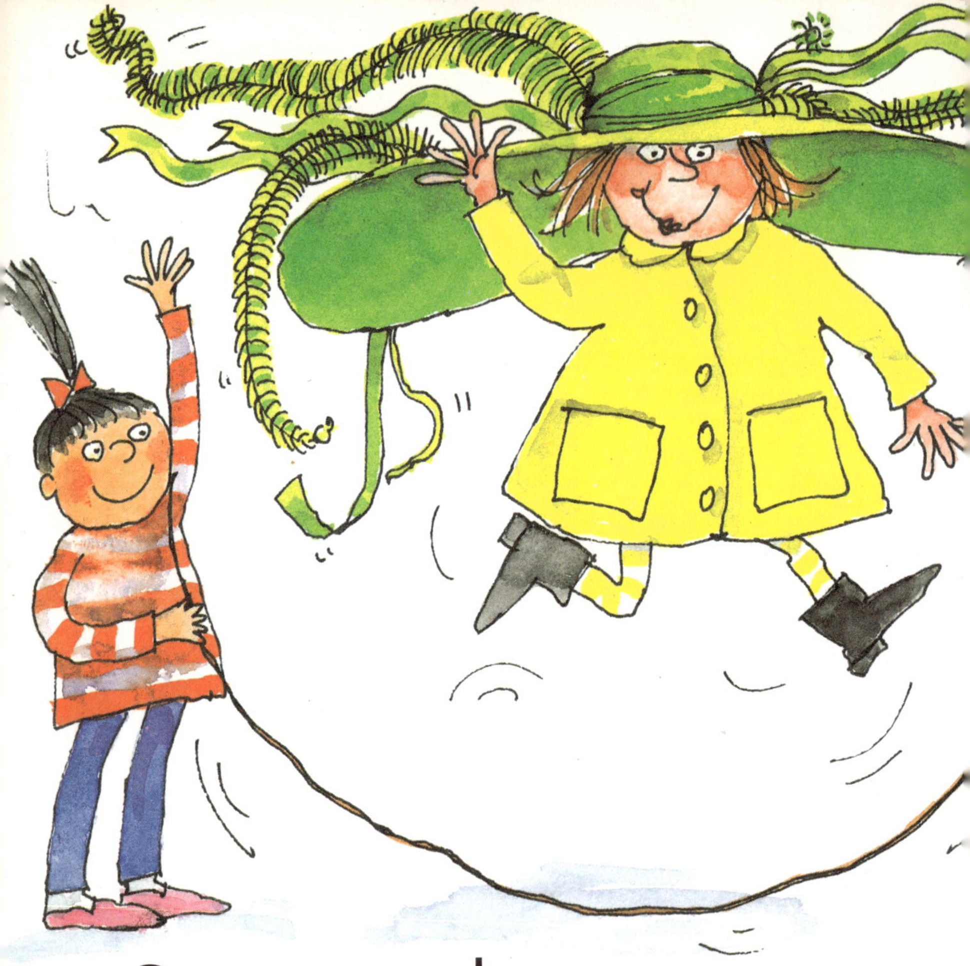

Out goes the woman
with the big green hat.

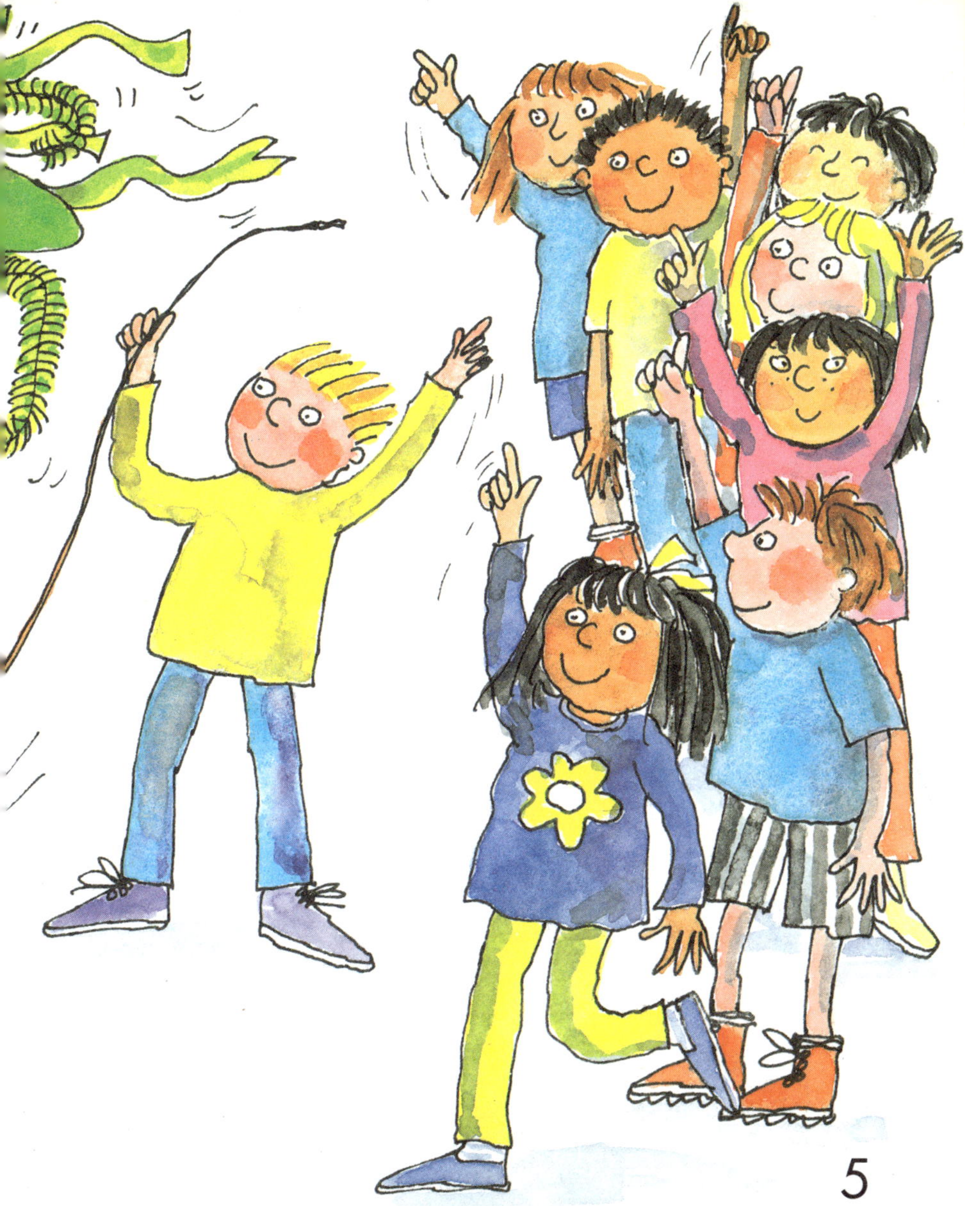

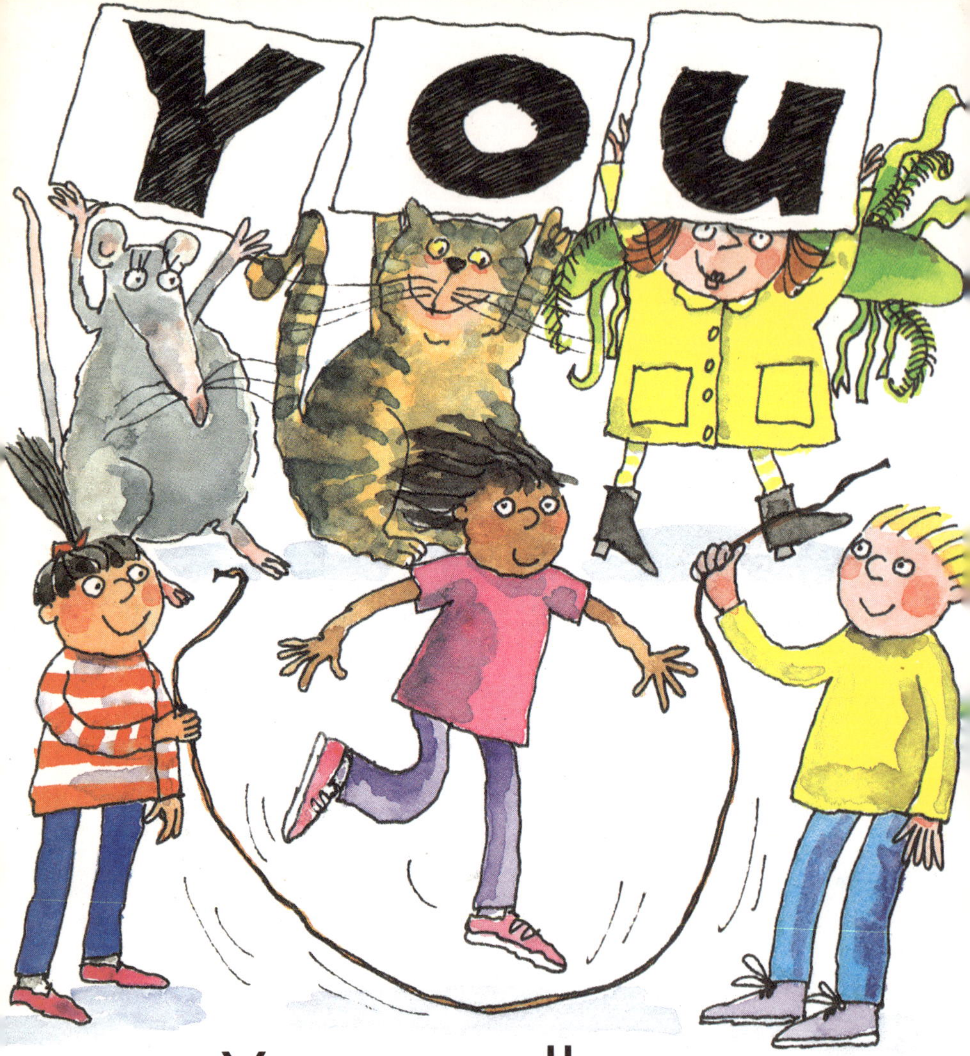

Y o u spells you.

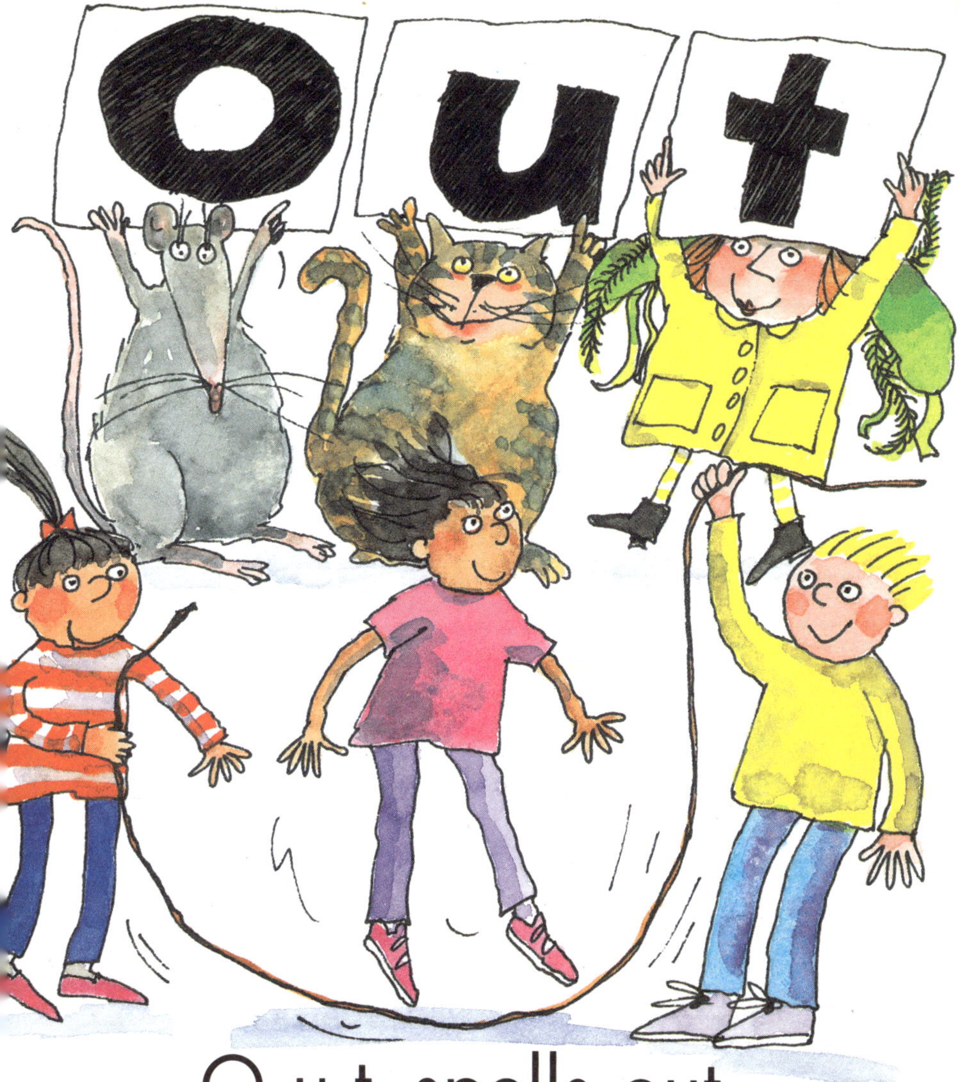

O u t spells out.

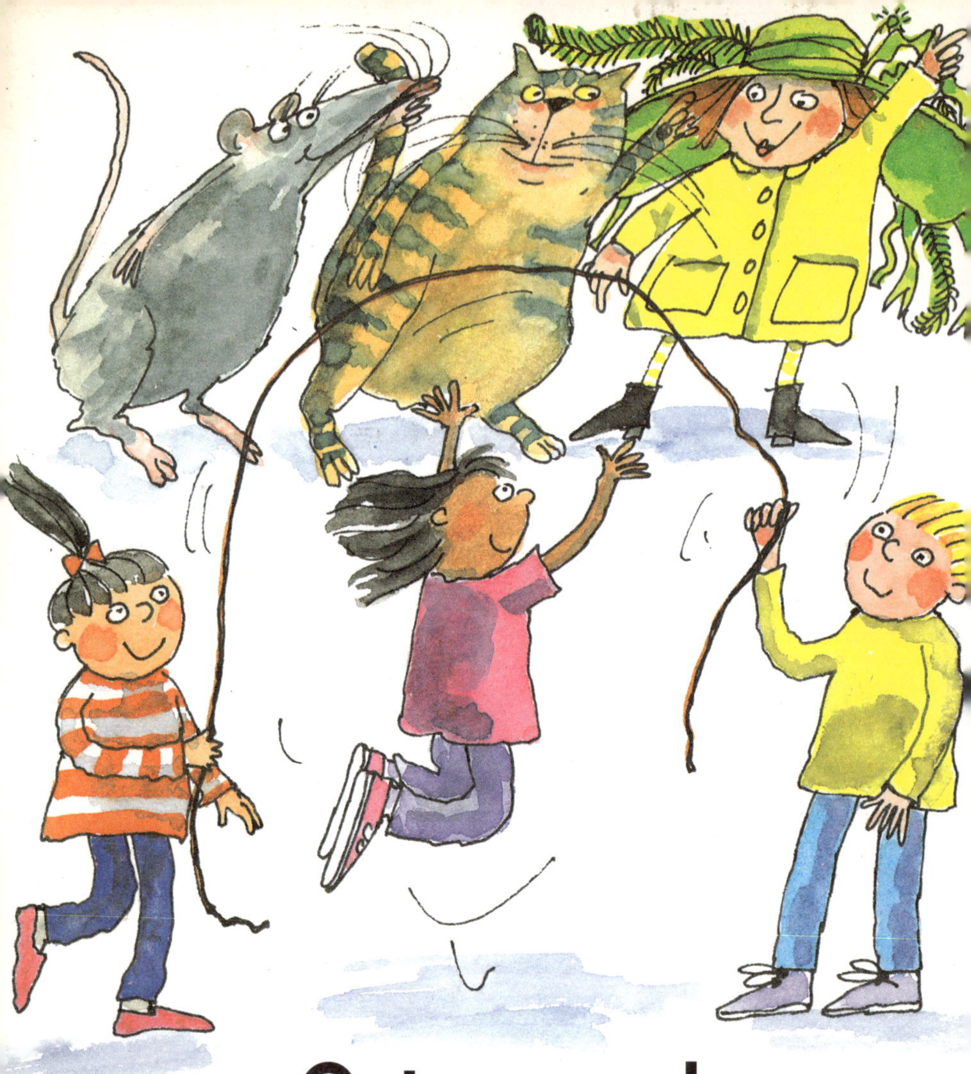

Out you go!